OFF-the-HOOK BIG BOOK OF REALLY DUMB SCHOOL JOKES

OFF-the-HOOK BIG BOOK OF REALLY DUMB SCHOOL JOKES

by Holly Kowitt

Illustrated by Donna Reynolds

SCHOLASTIC INC.
New York Toronto London Auckland Sydney
Mexico City New Delhi Hong Kong Buenos Aires

ISBN-10: 0-439-93335-8
ISBN-13: 978-0-439-93335-3

12 11 10 9 8 7 6 5 4 3 2   7 8 9 10 11 12/0

23

Printed in the U.S.A.
First Scholastic Printing, April 2007

This book
is dedicated to
Jason and
Fisher.

GETTING TO SCHOOL
MY SCHOOL BUS, ROUTE OR WRONG

When are school buses sad?
When their tires are low

Why did the mother pour water into her SUV?
She wanted to start a carpool.

Why couldn't the frog find his car?
It was toad.

What time is it when Godzilla catches your school bus?
Crush hour

Why couldn't the ghost take the bus?

He didn't have exact chains.

How did the comedian's son get to school?

In his jokeswagon

Who can hold up a school bus with one hand?

A crossing guard

Why did the driver throw clothes under the school bus?

He wanted a change of attire.

 # EXCUSES FOR BEING LATE TO SCHOOL

1. They're always ringing the bell before I get there.

2. I saw a sign that read SCHOOL AHEAD. GO SLOW. So I did.

3. My watch was set to Tokyo time.

4. I had to feed my pet piranha.

5. My alarm clock kept going off while I was asleep.

6. Sorry — usually, my punctuation skills are excellent.

7. I was dreaming about a basketball game, and it went into overtime.

8. *I'm* on time — everyone else is early.

9. I told you if I wasn't here, you should go ahead and start without me.

10. What? I thought this place was open until three thirty!

Why was the computer late to school?

It had a hard drive.

How is a school bus driver different from a cold?

One knows the stops, one stops the nose.

What kind of stories did the school bus driver tell?

Toll tales

What happened to the kid who missed the school bus?

He caught it when he came home.

Why did the dog sleep under the school bus?

He wanted to get up oily in the morning.

What do school bus drivers have for breakfast?
Traffic jam

Why didn't Jay ride his bike to school?
Because it was two-tired

KNOCK KNOCK.
Who's there?
RUSSIA
Russia who?
RUSSIA KID TO SCHOOL,
AND HE'LL FORGET HIS BOOKS!

KNOCK KNOCK.
Who's there?
MISTY
Misty who?
MISTY BUS, SO I HAVE TO WALK.

KNOCK KNOCK.
Who's there?
LUKE
Luke who?
LUKE OUT FOR THAT TRUCK!

TOP 10 THINGS YOU DON'T WANT TO HEAR FROM THE SCHOOL BUS DRIVER

1. I just thought it would be easier if we rotated drivers.

2. Right now I'm on an all-beans diet.

3. What does it mean when the dashboard is covered with red lights?

4. Don't worry. If a tire falls off, we have three others.

5. Sorry — the school wouldn't spend extra for seats.

6. This bus is shoes-optional.

7. Sure we can change the music — I have other Barry Manilow CDs.

8. They kicked me off the NASCAR tour.

9. If the police stop us, I'll do the talking.

10. Houston, we have a problem.

FAKING THE GRADE

THIS STUFF IS CLASSIFIED.

Why was the Xerox machine kicked out of school?

It copied.

Why did the teacher dunk her exam in the ocean?

She wanted to test the waters.

Why did the teacher carry birdseed?

She had a parrot-teacher conference.

How is school like a kid's toy?

There's always some assembly required.

Student: Can you help me out?

Teacher: Sure. Which way did you come in?

Why did the mall rat write her test answers in lipstick?

It was a makeup exam.

What do you give a teacher on the first day of school?

A supplies party

TOP 10 THINGS YOU'LL NEVER HEAR A TEACHER SAY

1. Keep shouting "No Homework," and I'll reconsider.

2. Who drew this picture of me on the blackboard? Well done!

3. Keep your cell phones on — I wouldn't want you to miss a call.

4. Turn up the volume, people!

5. I'd like you to get to a higher level of Mortal Kombat.

6. Tonight your assignment is to read four comic books and watch pro wrestling.

7. In real life, you'll never need to know algebra.

8. Usually I wouldn't accept a book report on the *Yu-Gi-Oh Trading Card Guide*, but yours is so well written, I'll make an exception.

9. Text your friends whenever you feel like it.

10. Homework can wait. You've got to finish reading that joke book.

What do young astronauts get on their homework?

Gold stars

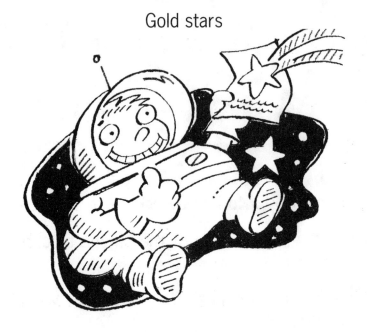

When can you learn something at a restaurant?

When there are several courses

Teacher: You aren't paying attention. Are you having trouble hearing?

Charlie: No, I'm having trouble listening.

Teacher: You're late again.

Willie: I couldn't find my homework.

Teacher: How about you, Randy?

Randy: I was copying it.

Teacher: How do you spell "Mississippi"?

Student: The river or the state?

Teacher: Your brain is an amazing organ.

Carla: Why?

Teacher: It starts working the minute you get up in the morning and doesn't stop until you're called on in class.

Teacher: Pamela, the essay you handed in about your cat is exactly like your brother's.

Pamela: Well, it's the same cat.

What do farmers like about school?

Field trips

WHERE DID THEY GO TO SCHOOL?

. . . King Arthur?
Knight School

. . . the ice-cream vendor?
Sundae School

. . . the X-treme sports fan?
Boarding school

. . . the geologist?
School of Rock

. . . the belly dancer?
The Navel Academy

. . . Sherlock Holmes?
Elementary

Teacher: Tommy, what is our gross national product?

Tommy: Broccoli?

Mother: What did you learn in school?

Arnold: Our teacher taught us to write.

Mother: What did you write?

Arnold: I don't know. We haven't learned how to read.

Teacher: Do you know what an echo is?

Emma: Could you repeat the question?

Mom: Why did you fail that quiz?

Peter: Because of absence.

Mom: You were absent that day?

Peter: No, the girl who sits next to me was.

Did the pizza do well at college?

Yes — it was Pie Beta Kappa.

Dumb: Why are you eating your math test?

Dumber: The teacher said it was

a piece of cake.

Patty: How did you get so black-and-blue?

Matty: From all the class trips!

What happens when the teacher is sick at the Naval Academy?

They hire a sub.

How do you mail a package to a teacher?

First class

Where can monsters find out how their kids do in school?

A parent-creature conference

Teacher: What's the second to last letter of the alphabet?

Maria: Y.

Teacher: Because I want to know.

Teacher: Sometimes, I think you don't listen to a word I say!

Student: What?

Why did the tree flunk its math test?

It was stumped.

Why did the police search the boring teacher's classroom?

They'd heard there'd been a kid napping.

Kid: I'd like an apple for my teacher.

Grocer: Sorry, we don't do trades.

Teacher: Here is your report card.

Ben: I don't want to scare you, but my dad said if I didn't get good grades, somebody was going to get spanked.

Teacher: Anne, how do you spell rain?

Anne: R-A-N-E.

Teacher: That's the worst spell of rain we've had in a while.

Teacher: Can you name the seven continents?

Phil: I don't have to. They've already been named.

Teacher: What's going on here?

Philip: Tommy threw a spitball at me,
so I threw one back.

Teacher: Why didn't you come to me?

Philip: Your aim isn't as good as mine.

Why did the geography student flunk out?

She had a bad latitude.

**Caitlin: Did you know girls
are smarter than boys?**

Tyler: No.

Caitlin: See what I mean?

**Mother: It says here that you're ranked at the
bottom in a class of 25. That's awful.**

Son: It could be worse.

Mother: How?

Son: The class could have been bigger.

TOP TEN NO-FAIL HOMEWORK EXCUSES

TOP 10

1. My mom baked it into the Tofu Surprise.

2. My dad used it to housebreak our puppy.

3. Teachers are overworked, and I didn't want to contribute to that.

4. You already collected it. . . . Don't tell me you *lost* it!

5. Jeter was sick, so the Yankees asked me to fill in.

6. Our house burned down, and we needed it for tissues.

7. The President asked to borrow it for a summit meeting.

8. Watch the swinging pendulum and repeat after me: There was *no* assignment.

9. The aliens have asked me not to discuss it.

10. I thought you said, "May 18, 2020."

TOP 10 REJECTED THEMES FOR SCHOOL DANCES

1. Evening in the Gym

2. See Your Math Teacher Do the Robot

3. Get Rejected Under the Stars

4. Our Friend the Flatworm

5. 1,001 Polka Hits

6. Like Science Class, But with Music

7. Acne and Fruit Punch

8. The Life and Times of Millard Fillmore

9. Hooked on Phonics

10. The Girl You Like Still Won't Talk to You

KNOCK KNOCK.
Who's there?
BORIS.
Boris who?
BORIS WITH A LECTURE –
I COULD USE THE SLEEP.

KNOCK KNOCK.
Who's there?
PENCIL.
Pencil who?
PENCIL FALL DOWN IF
YOU DON'T WEAR A BELT.

KNOCK KNOCK.
Who's there?
CHALK.
Chalk who?
CHALK TO ME, BABY!

KNOCK KNOCK.
Who's there?
JUAN.
Juan who?
JUAN TO GO TO THE DANCE WITH ME?

KNOCK KNOCK.
Who's there?
JOYCE.
Joyce who?
MULTIPLE JOYCE TESTS ARE EASIER.

KNOCK KNOCK.
Who's there?
DETENTION.
Detention who?
DE TENSION IN DIS ROOM IS KILLING ME!

KNOCK KNOCK.
Who's there?
DIPLOMA.
Diploma who?
DIPLOMA'S COMING TO FIX DE SINK.

Beth: Why are you gluing yourself to that book?

Seth: The teacher said to stick to one subject.

Teacher: You play chess with your dog?
He must be very smart.

Rob: Not really. I beat him most of the time.

Why is Alabama the smartest state?

It has four A's and one B!

What did the Post-it note say to the paper?

"This is a stickup!"

THE SCHOOL BULLY

How did the school bully get everyone's lunch money?

He stayed calm and collected.

Why did the bully take off his watch?

Because time will tell

What time is it when the basketball team chases after a bully?

Five after one

Where did they put the lunchroom bully?

Behind salad bars

Why don't bullies become farmers?

Because pigs squeal

What happened when the bully hid stolen money in his mouth?

He had two buck teeth.

What did the bully get from the astronaut?

Launch money

Bully: Give me a dollar for a sandwich.

Howard: Okay, but it won't taste very good.

A bully wrote this e-mail to a classmate:

Gue$$ what I want? $ee me $oon.

His classmate wrote back:

NOthing new here. Just aNOther day . . .

Bye 4 NOw.

TOP 10 THINGS TO SAY TO THE SCHOOL BULLY

1. I'd like to fight you, but I'm booked till 2025.

2. It'll be nice to fight someone other than karate black belts.

3. I can't fight you until my mad cow disease clears up.

4. If you break my fingers, I can't do your homework for you.

5. I forgot my lunch money at home, along with my Death Ray 2000 stun gun.

6. I'll have to make it quick, because my football team will be here any minute.

7. Sorry, all my money goes to aliens from planet Zorbleck.

8. Hold on a sec — this call is from the last kid I sent to the hospital.

9. I warn you: I throw up when I'm scared.

10. I'll catch up with you later — after my Sopranos family reunion.

THE SCHOOL CAFETERIA

LOSE YOUR LUNCH.

Did you hear about the cafeteria lady who backed up into the meat grinder?

She got a little behind in her work.

Boy: From now on, I'm eating only greens.

Girl: Really? Can I have the other M&M's?

Mom: I know what you ate for lunch. Sloppy Joe, orange juice, and chocolate cake.

Mark: You saw the menu?

Mom: No, I saw your shirt.

What did the caveman order at the school cafeteria?

A clubbed sandwich

Peter: There's a dead bug in my gravy!

Andy: He must have committed insecticide.

Why did the boy bring scissors to the cafeteria?

He wanted to cut the lunch line.

What's the happiest dessert in the lunchroom?

Cheery pie

Why did the student give his giant sandwich to the birds?

It was too much tweet.

TOP 10 THINGS YOU DON'T WANT TO HEAR IN THE SCHOOL CAFETERIA

1. Didn't they serve this meal on *Survivor*?

2. It's *probably* apple cider.

3. Hey, Wanda — someone ordered the prune cobbler!

4. Has anyone seen my scab collection?

5. I don't know how old the mystery chow mein is. I've only worked here three weeks.

6. We're asking everyone to wear a hazmat suit today.

7. Delivery! Where do I put this box of pigs' feet?

8. Hey, I've never seen you at the "cool" table before!

9. The mashed potatoes are green for St. Patrick's Day, right?

10. What do you mean the lettuce hasn't been washed? You can still see the soap on it!

What's the school basketball team doing for breakfast?

Dunkin' donuts

Cafeteria worker: Why do you keep spitting up your food?

Steve: I thought you might want some feedback.

Ryan: What's that in my pudding?

Cafeteria worker: Ask your science teacher.

I can't tell one insect from another.

What's a teacher's favorite flavor?

Chalk-olate

How do they prevent crime in the lunchroom?

With a burger alarm

MOVIES SHOWN IN THE SCHOOL CAFETERIA

PIE-RATES OF THE CARIBBEAN
THE SPONGECAKE SQUAREPANTS MOVIE
MISSION: IM-PASTA-BLE
THE LION, THE SANDWICH, AND THE WARDROBE
ELVIS PARSLEY MOVIE MARATHON
LORD OF THE JELL-O RINGS
CHERRY POTTER AND THE SORCERER'S SCONE

Two students waited in line at the school lunch counter.

"What can I get you to drink?" asked the cafeteria worker.

"Apple juice, please," said one student.

"Me too," said the other kid. "And make sure I get a clean glass."

The cafeteria worker returned with their drinks. "Right. Now which one of you asked for the clean glass?"

Terry: The good thing about the school cafeteria is we can eat dirt cheap.

Mary: Who wants to eat dirt?

Tiffany: Two complaints. First of all, the food here is awful.

Cafeteria worker: I'm sorry. What's the other complaint?

Tiffany: The portions are too small!

Don: Can I have meat loaf without ketchup?

Cafeteria worker: We're all out of ketchup.

But I can give it to you without mustard.

What kind of candy do you eat during playtime?

Recess pieces

Student: Is this tuna casserole or chili con carne?

Cafeteria worker:
Can't you tell by the taste?

Student: No, I can't!

Cafeteria worker:
Then what difference does it make?

SIGNS YOU'VE EATEN TOO MUCH

You've broken two cafeteria chairs.

You can't leave the lunchroom until they widen the door.

You ate the fish sticks, the fork, and the paper plate.

You just lost your cell phone in your lap.

You're sweating chocolate milk.

What did the kid say when he dropped his cafeteria tray?

"Lunch is on me!"

How did the eggs get on the honor roll?

They were Grade A.

What did the candy lover ask the dentist?

"Can I have a crème filling?"

The cafeteria worker handed the student a hot dog with her thumb pressed down on it. The student was horrified. "Why are you putting your hand on my food?" she asked. "So it doesn't fall on the floor again," said the cafeteria worker.

What did one hamburger say to another?
"Nice buns!"

What happened to the girl who drank 8 sodas?
She burped 7-up.

Why wouldn't the potato chips listen to the sandwich?
It was full of bologna!

Why did the school chef put mouthwash in the gazpacho?
So it wouldn't have bad broth

How do you fix a broken pizza?
With tomato paste

What do you eat when there's an elephant in the lunchroom?

Squash

Should you eat fish sticks with your fingers?

No, fish sticks should be eaten with tartar sauce.

KNOCK KNOCK.

Who's there?

MR. E.

Mr. E. who?

MYSTERY MEAT FOR LUNCH AGAIN!

KNOCK KNOCK.

Who's there?

DISHES.

Dishes who?

DISHES THE WORST MEAT LOAF I EVER ATE!

KNOCK KNOCK.

Who's there?

PUDDING.

Pudding who?

PUDDING KETCHUP ON IT WON'T HELP!

KNOCK KNOCK.

Who's there?

BUTTER.

Butter who?

BUTTER NOT HAVE THE LASAGNA!

KNOCK KNOCK.

Who's there?

WOODEN.

Wooden who?

WOODEN EAT THE
CHILI IF I WERE YOU.

THIS WEEK'S SCHOOL CAFETERIA MENU*

MONDAY

Washroom Barley Soup
Meat Con Carne
Reek Salad
Fish Ticks
Lint Chocolate Chip Ice Cream

TUESDAY

Mystery Tacos
Selection of Old Cuts
Hurried Chicken Salad
Spit Pea Soup
Coffee with Nutra-Sweat (Teachers only)

WEDNESDAY

One-ton Soup
Vegetarian Steak
Rot Dogs and Hurly Fries
Beef Spew
Chicken à la Thing
Hot sludge sundae

THURSDAY

Spaghetti and Hairballs
Burger with Flies
Key Slime Pie
Iced Flea

FRIDAY

Hamburger Splatter
Tuna Smelt
Shrimp Jell-O
Faked Potato
Rocky Roadkill Ice Cream

*All entrees served with your choice
of noodles or lice

During lunch hour, students are asked
not to heave the table.

TOP 10 SIGNS YOUR SCHOOL CAFETERIA FOOD IS LOUSY

1. You eat something pretty good, then realize it's the paper plate.

2. You cut your hand on the Jell-O.

3. The meat loaf comes with a saw.

4. No one minded the school power outage because they couldn't see what they were eating.

5. Even the teachers have food fights.

6. The coffee was ground this morning — literally.

7. Your hamburger has a tail.

8. The sponge cake is made of actual sponge.

9. Before you eat, you have to sign a paper promising not to sue.

10. The kindergarten turtle is looking pretty tasty right now.

SOME RESPONSES TO THE COMPLAINT: "THERE'S A FLY IN MY SOUP!"

"DON'T WORRY— WE WON'T CHARGE EXTRA!"

"SHHHHH, THE OTHER STUDENTS WILL WANT ONE, TOO."

"HMMM . . . THERE WERE TWO OF THEM WHEN I SERVED YOU!"

"IT'S OKAY—IT DOESN'T EAT TOO MUCH."

"AT LEAST IT'S NOT HALF A FLY, IF YOU KNOW WHAT I MEAN."

"I KNOW. LOOK AT IT DIVE FOR THE SPINACH."

"DON'T WORRY— THERE'S A SPIDER ON THE BREAD."

"HEY—NO PETS ALLOWE IN SCHOOL!"

MONSTERS IN SCHOOL

YOU GO, GHOUL!

What did the executioner do at the mall?

His back-to-school chopping

What does a wizard use to grade quizzes?

A magic marker

What does Godzilla eat when he goes to the school cafeteria?

The school cafeteria

Where do zombies go before middle school?

Grave school

What sport do mummies go out for?

Casketball

What did the zombie like about school?

Stiff competition

Why don't skeletons like school dances?

They have no body to go with.

What aren't witches allowed to do in class?

Hex messaging

Who do zombies go to the prom with?

Whoever they can dig up

Why did Dracula get sent to the school nurse?

Because of his coffin

Why did the school hire a ghost as a groundskeeper?

They needed someone to moan the lawn.

Is it hard to clean a haunted locker?

No, dirt and grime just vanish.

How does the Cyclops listen to music?

On an Eye-pod

Do mummies like school?

Of corpse!

Why was the monster kicked out of class?

His eyes were on someone else's paper.

What's a little witch's favorite subject?

Spelling

Did you hear about the skull who teaches science?

He's the department head.

Why do witches like the school cafeteria?

Because they serve big potions

Why did the vampire flunk out of school?

He had a bat attitude.

What grade did the Headless Horseman get?

Incomplete

KNOCK KNOCK.
Who's there?
GHOST.
Ghost who?
THE GHOST IS CLEAR — LET'S RUN!

KNOCK KNOCK.
Who's there?
WITCH.
Witch who?
WITCH YOU LET ME IN ALREADY?

KNOCK KNOCK.
Who's there?
CRYPT.
Crypt who?
CRYPT UP SO I COULD SCARE YOU.

KNOCK KNOCK.
Who's there?
CLAWS.
Claws who?
CLAWS THE DOOR —
THERE'S WEREWOLVES AROUND!

KNOCK KNOCK.
Who's there?
GOBLIN.
Goblin who?
GOBBLIN' MY LUNCH BEFORE IT ESCAPES!

KNOCK KNOCK.
Who's there?
WEIRDO.
Weirdo who?
WEIRDO YOU GET SUCH TERRIBLE KNOCK KNOCKS?

WHY DID THEY FLUNK OUT?

THE GHOST?
He wouldn't stay in his sheet.

THE BLOB?
It couldn't keep its mouths shut.

THE INVISIBLE MAN?
Teacher always marks him absent.

THE ZOMBIE?
He wanted to go to an all-ghouls school.

THE ABOMINABLE SNOWMAN?
His work wasn't so hot.

THE DECOMPOSING CORPSE?
His grades were rotten.

CLASSY ANSWERS TO DUMB QUESTIONS

ARE YOU SLEEPING IN CLASS?

⇨ No, I'm just using my head to hold

my desk down.

⇨ Why, is my snoring keeping others awake?

⇨ I forgot to do it during science.

ARE YOU TALKING ON A CELL PHONE?

⇨ No, I'm exercising my arms with some free weights.

⇨ No, psychotic people often talk to themselves.

⇨ No, I'm using a mind control device

for teachers. Can you dismiss us from class?

WHY DON'T YOU TAKE OUT YOUR MATH BOOK?

⇨ Okay — how about dinner and a movie?

⇨ I'm already dating someone.

⇨ It has too many problems.

DID YOU TAKE THE BUS?

⇨ Why? Is one missing?

⇨ No, I thought the Good Humor truck would be faster.

⇨ Yes, but I've been meaning to give it back.

WHY DID YOU MISS SCHOOL YESTERDAY?

⇨ I didn't miss it at all.

⇨ I'm doing my part to relieve school overcrowding.

⇨ I guess my aim is lousy.

WHAT DID YOU LEARN IN SCHOOL TODAY?

⇨ Not enough. I have to go back tomorrow.

⇨ When you copy off someone, don't put her name

on your paper.

⇨ The ride is better on top of the bus.

ADULTS ANSWER BACK

Are you serving meatballs today?

☆ YES, WE'LL SERVE ANYONE.

☆ NO, WE JUST DIDN'T KNOW HOW TO SPELL "FILET MIGNON."

☆ NO, WE'RE SERVING MOON ROCKS. THEY'RE METEOR.

Are you a substitute?

☆ NO, ONE OF THESE DAYS I'LL PASS FIFTH GRADE.

☆ NO, I'M YOUR REGULAR TEACHER DRESSED UP
FOR HALLOWEEN.

☆ NO, I'M A SUPERMODEL. IS THIS THE
CALVIN KLEIN COMMERCIAL?

Do we have homework tonight?

☆ NO, TONIGHT I'M ASSIGNING HOUSEWORK.

☆ NO, WE HAVE GNOME-WORK — FOR ALL THE
TROLLS IN CLASS.

☆ YES, YOUR ASSIGNMENT IS TO STUDY THE EFFECT
OF PIZZA ON THE HUMAN APPETITE.

Am I late?

☆ NOT FOR TOMORROW'S CLASS.

☆ NO, THAT LOUD BELL WAS FROM THE PRINCIPAL'S BICYCLE.

☆ HMMM, I THOUGHT YOU WERE JASON.

Did you like that book, *Off-the-Hook Big Book of Really Dumb School Jokes*?

☆ SCHOOL JOKES? I THOUGHT IT WAS THE COMPLETE
   WORKS OF WILLIAM SHAKESPEARE.

☆ AS A BOOK, NO, BUT AS A POOPER-SCOOPER,
   IT WAS EXCELLENT.

☆ NO, EXCEPT THE PART THAT READ, "THE END."

LOSER FRIENDLY

AN APPLE FOR THE TEACHER, AND OTHER COMPUTER SPAM

What did the computer do at the beach?

It put on some screen saver and surfed the net.

Why did the hacker bring a cockroach to the gym?

He had a few bugs to work out.

Ben: I wish I had enough money to buy the world's most expensive computer.

Jen: Why do you want the world's most expensive computer?

Ben: I don't. I just want the money.

What did the hacker order at McDonald's?

A Big iMac

Why did the starving man break open his computer?

He heard there were chips inside.

Why did the computer screen go to school?

It wanted to be a hall monitor.

Why did the hackers go the school nurse?

They had bad codes.

TOP 10 SIGNS YOU BOUGHT A BAD COMPUTER

1. It comes with a one-hour warranty.

2. A sticker on the bottom reads MADE IN OCCUPIED JAPAN.

3. To start it, you need jumper cables.

4. The keyboard doesn't have any letters you recognize.

5. The only chips inside are Pringles.

6. The manual says when it freezes, wrap it in a sweater.

7. You can't get on the Internet, but you can microwave popcorn.

8. It's made of wood.

9. On closer inspection, you realize the apple logo is actually a lemon.

10. An adult can operate it.

Why wouldn't the cleaning lady dust the computer?

She doesn't do windows.

Mother: I'm sorry, but you have to turn off that computer. You sit in front of it all day and don't hear anything I say. You don't even answer when I talk, do you?

Son:

Neighbor: Godzilla, how do you like your new computer?

Godzilla: With a little bit of ketchup.

Why did the boy double his computer's salary?

Because it quit unexpectedly

Why didn't the hacker do his homework?

He was saving it for a brainy day.

TOP 10 LEAST POPULAR VIDEO GAMES

1. X-treme Mall Walking

2. Weeding the Garden

3. Alien Podiatrist

4. Reach for Your Slippers

5. Gangsta Birdbath II

6. Slug Race

7. Battle of the Beanie Babies

8. Eat Your Croissant

9. Grand Theft Auto: Iowa

10. Mortal Kroquet

THE SCHOOL NURSE
THESE JOKES ARE SICK.

Wendy: Nurse, my brother just stepped in front of the school bus!

Nurse: So he's got that run-down feeling . . . ?

Student: Nurse, I think I have a food problem.

Nurse: Why?

Student: Five hours after I eat, I'm hungry again!

Student: Nurse, I just swallowed my cell phone. What should I do?

Nurse: Use a pay phone.

Freddie: Will these stairs take me to the nurse's office?

Eddie: No, you have to climb them.

Student: Can you help me? At night I snore so loudly, I wake myself up.

Nurse: In that case, you should sleep in another room.

Carl: My brother copies everything I do!

Nurse: Why is he acting like an idiot?

Student: What's the best thing to do for mosquito bites?

Nurse: Don't bite any.

Why did the chimney go to the nurse?

It had the flue.

Student: Well, how am I?

Nurse: Well, there's good news and bad news.

Student: What's the good news?

Nurse: After testing you for everything, I can't find anything wrong with you.

Student: Good. So what's the bad news?

Nurse: I'm not a real nurse.

Teacher: Nurse, did you take this student's temperature?

Nurse: No, is it missing?

Student: Nurse, nurse, I'm shrinking!

Nurse: Oh, be a little patient.

Student: Nurse! Nurse! No one pays attention to me.

Nurse: Next!

Why did the toilet go to the school nurse?

It was feeling flushed.

Nurse: How did you break your foot?

Kyle: I dropped some peas on it.

Nurse: Peas? How could peas do that?

Kyle: They were in a can.

Student: Nurse, I broke my leg in two places!

Nurse: Well, don't go back to either one.

Student: Nurse, my foot falls asleep every night.

Nurse: What's wrong with that?

Student: It's snoring!

Teacher: How's that kid who swallowed his lunch money?

Nurse: No change yet.

Why did the pony go to the nurse?

It was a little hoarse.

Nurse: I'd like to take out your splinter.

Hank: Okay, but have it back by midnight.

 # REASONS NOT TO GO TO THE SCHOOL NURSE

1. A bad case of hat head

2. Rug burn

3. Foosball finger

4. Ice-cream headache

5. Pulled eyebrow

6. Sprained earlobe

7. Algebra-phobia

8. Urge to hoard tongue depressors for craft projects

9. Bruised ego

10. Terminal embarrassment

THE SCHOOL PSYCHOLOGIST

JUST TESTING

Student: Doctor, I think I'm a bridge!

School psychologist: What's come
over you lately?

Student: Doctor, I keep thinking I'm a dog.

School psychologist: Sit down on the couch
and we'll talk.

Student: But I'm not allowed on the couch!

Student: Doctor, I get the feeling people don't care about anything I say.

School psychologist: So?

School psychologist: What brings you to my office?

Student: I think I'm a pair of curtains.

School psychologist: Well, pull yourself together.

Student: Doctor, I feel like a deck of cards.

School psychologist: I'll deal with you later.

Student: Doctor, I have this problem. Half the time I think I'm a wigwam, the other half I think I'm a tepee.

School psychologist: Relax. You're two tents.

Student: Doctor, I'm starting to think I'm a phone cord.

School psychologist: We'll straighten you out.

TOP 10 THINGS TO SAY TO A SUBSTITUTE TEACHER

1. In our class, tests are optional.

2. Lunch lasts from eleven to two.

3. Our school cafeteria is in the mall across the street.

4. Instead of grades, our teacher gives us money.

5. That loud rap music is coming from the PA system.

6. We leave cell phones on in case our parents call.

7. Gold stars are given to people who spell their name right.

8. Each class holds its own fire drill.

9. This is Whiskers, the class ferret.

10. *WWE Smackdown was* our class assignment!

GEE . . . OGRAPHY!

JOIN THE COUNTRY CLUB.

What country can you eat dinner on?

China

What did Sweden say when its next-door neighbor proposed?

Norway!

Where do you find sharks?

Finland

Where can you always get take-out food?

Togo

What country never stands up?
Lapland

Who's always ready to eat?
Hungary

What country is square?
Cuba

Where do you go for Thanksgiving?
Turkey

Hey, man, do you like small, Middle Eastern countries?
Yemen

Where do frogs come from?
Greenland

What country wears a suit?
Thailand

What country left quickly?
Iran

What country catches colds?
Germany

What country likes to sunbathe?
Tanzania

What country can you cook bacon in?
Greece

What country is always cold?
Chile

What country doesn't use cash?
The Czech Republic

KNOCK KNOCK
Who's there?
SUMATRA.
Sumatra who?
NOTHING. WHAT'S SUMATRA WITH YOU?

KNOCK KNOCK.
Who's there?
KENYA.
Kenya who?
KENYA GIMME YOUR LUNCH MONEY?

KNOCK KNOCK.
Who's there?
SAMOA.
Samoa who?
SAMOA MUSTARD, PLEASE.

KNOCK KNOCK.
Who's there?
GHANA.
Ghana who?
GHANA GET ICE CREAM NOW.

KNOCK KNOCK.
Who's there?
JAMAICA.
Jamaica who?
JAMAICA GIVE YOU HER PICKLE?

KNOCK KNOCK.
Who's there?
KUWAIT.
Kuwait who?
KUWAIT UNTIL I'VE FINISHED
MY KNOCK KNOCK JOKE?

ANIMALS IN SCHOOL
GOPHER IT.

Why did the dog wear a cap and gown?

He was picking up his master's degree.

**What do you call an alligator
with three tests to study for?**

Swamped!

Why can't leopards cheat on tests?

Because they're always spotted

Where does a sheep carry its books?

In its baaaaackpack

Why were the elephants kicked off the swim team?

They were walking around with their trunks down.

Why did the rabbit teachers go on strike?

They wanted a better celery.

Why wasn't the grizzly allowed in the cafeteria?

He had bear feet.

Why did the stegosaurus make the volleyball team?

It knows how to spike the ball!

What is a lion's favorite time in history?

The civil roar

What grade do you give a horse?

Hay-plus

What did the buffalo say when his boy went off to college?

"Bison!"

Why did the bald teacher put a rabbit on his head?

He needed the hare.

What do chickens study for?

Eggs-ams!

Why is it hard to give an exam in the jungle?

Too many cheetahs

KNOCK KNOCK.
Who's there?
SHEEP.
Sheep who?
SHEEP AT HOME, NOT IN CLASS!

KNOCK KNOCK.
Who's there?
AARDVARK.
Aardvark who?
AARDVARK TO SCHOOL, BUT I'D BE LATE.

KNOCK KNOCK.
Who's there?
RHINO.
Rhino who?
RHINO THE ANSWER –
CALL ON ME!

KNOCK KNOCK.
Who's there?
IGUANA.
Iguana who?
IGUANA GET A WEDGIE IF THE BULLY SEES ME.

 # ANIMALS READING LIST

1. *Harry Otter*

2. *The Magic School Buzz*

3. *Goodnight Moooon*

4. *Little Mouse on the Prairie*

5. *Harriet the Fly*

6. *Red Badger of Courage*

7. *James and the Giant Pooch*

8. *The Phantomcat Tollbooth*

9. *Mongoosebumps*

10. *Moby Duck*

BEE STUDENTS
CREEPY CRAWLIES GO TO SCHOOL.

Why did the snake walk home from school?
Because it hissed the bus

Why did the teacher excuse the firefly?
Because when you gotta glow, you gotta glow

Why did the hornet go to music school?
He wanted to be a stinger-songwriter.

How was the snake greeted at assembly?
They gave him a worm welcome.

What kind of school did the queen bee attend?
Buzz-ness school

What kinds of insects spend all their time together?

Best bugs

What do butterflies learn in school?

Moth-e-matics

KNOCK KNOCK.

Who's there?

TOAD.

Toad who?

TOAD YOU WE WERE HAVING FLIES FOR LUNCH!

KNOCK KNOCK.
Who's there?
BEEHIVE.
Beehive who?
BEEHIVE YOURSELF!

KNOCK KNOCK.
Who's there?
ROACH.
Roach who?
ROACH YOU A LETTER,
BUT YOU DIDN'T ANSWER!

KNOCK KNOCK.
Who's there?
LICE.
Lice who?
LICE TO MEET YOU, TOO!

THE ALL-PURPOSE GET-OUT-OF-SCHOOL EXCUSE

Dear Mr./Mrs./Ms._____,
     [circle]

Please excuse _____ from school for the next _____ days.
            [your name]   [number]

He/she has come down with a bad case of the _____-an flu and
[circle]   [exotic country]

his/her entire body is covered in _____s. He/she is having difficulty
[circle]   [noun]   [circle]

_____-ing, especially during the hours of 8:30 to 3:15.
   [verb]

If he/she doesn't stay in bed with plenty of gummy _____s (for
[circle]   [animal]

medicinal purposes), he/she could be a ____ for the rest of his/her life.
                  [circle]   [noun]   [circle]

Hopefully, _____ will be up and about soon, when he/she has
       [name]   [circle]

watched enough reruns of _____.
              [TV show]

Sincerely,
[indecipherable signature]

P.S. Please DON'T mention this when you see me at the next school
event. And please don't call; I'm busy for the next _____ years.
                                        [high number]

DRESS CODE
WE'RE PUTTING YOU ON.

Who wears lots of clothes at once?
The student body

Why did the class president wear jogging shorts?
She wanted to run for office.

Who's the best dressed animal in school?
The porcupine — he always looks sharp!

Why did the mall rat bring a charge card to class?
She wanted extra credit.

On the field trip, what did the teacher wear under her dress?

A permission slip

What's a shirt's favorite phone service?

Collar ID

Melissa: I want to try on those pants in the window.

Store clerk: I'm sorry, you'll have to use the dressing room.

What do you get when pelicans go school shopping?

A big bill

Felicia: Whenever I'm down in the dumps, I buy new shoes.

Polly: So that's where you get them!

Why did the girl wear loud socks to school?

To keep from falling asleep

What do cafeteria workers wear on their feet?

Meat loafers

Teacher: Arielle, you're wearing mismatched socks.

Arielle: I know. And I have another pair just like them at home.

Mom: Want to come window shopping with me today?

Gwen: Great! What are we looking for?

Mom: Some windows.

KNOCK KNOCK.
Who's there?
SLEEVE.
Sleeve who?
SLEEVE ME ALONE!

KNOCK KNOCK.
Who's there?
A SHOE.
A shoe who?
GESUNDHEIT!

IT'S GEEK TO ME
SCIENCE JOKES

What was the geekiest dinosaur?

The pterodorktyl

How many ears do Trekkies have?

A left ear, a right ear, and the final front ear

Why couldn't the skunk do his chemistry experiment?

His mother didn't want him to stink up the house.

Why did the storm cloud follow the taxi?

It wanted to hail a cab.

Teacher: What is the chemical formula for water?

David: HIJKLMNO.

Teacher: What?

David: You said it was H to O!

What did the magnet say to the refrigerator?

"I find you very attractive."

How do amoebas keep in touch?

By cell phone.

Jack: They laughed when Edison invented the steamboat.

Mac: Fulton invented the steamboat.

Jack: No wonder they laughed.

Teacher: Why are dinosaurs extinct?

Olivia: Because they smell bad!

Teacher: What does it mean when the barometer is falling?

Hudson: It means whoever nailed it up
didn't do a good job.

Why do scientists like baseball?

They like looking at slides.

Teacher: What travels faster, heat or cold?

Gary: Heat. You can always catch a cold.

Karl: When I die, I'm going to leave my brain to science.

Stephanie: Good. Every little bit helps.

What color is the wind?

Blew.

KNOCK KNOCK.

Who's there?

PASTEUR.

Pasteur who?

PASTEUR BEDTIME, ISN'T IT?

KNOCK KNOCK.

Who's there?

WATER.

Water who?

WATER YOU DOING HERE?

LOONIER LANDINGS
OUT OF THIS WORLD

Why did the planet join the solar system?

He'd always wanted a sun.

What did one star say to another?

"You glow, girl!"

Science teacher: How many planets are in the sky?

Ben: All of them!

Rob: Someday I'll fly on a rocket to the sun.

Teacher: But the sun's so hot, you'll burn up.

Rob: That's why I'm going at night.

What did Cameron win for finding the Big Dipper?

A constellation prize

What do astronauts listen to on their iPods?

Neptunes

What did Saturn say to Jupiter?

"I'll give you a ring sometime!"

Why did the star go to the bathroom?

It had to twinkle.

DUMB AND DUMBER

HOW DUMB IS HE?

He flunked recess.

He went cordless bungee-jumping.

He thought Karl Marx was one of the Marx Brothers.

He thought the English Channel was between HBO and Nickelodeon.

He thought Harrison Ford invented the automobile.

He went to a drive-in to see "Closed for Winter."

He tried to buy a garage at a garage sale.

He tore out a page from his calendar because he wanted to take a month off.

The three best years of his life were fifth grade.

HOW DUMB IS SHE?

She threw a ball on the ground and missed.

She had to cheat to get an F.

She got her gold medal bronzed.

She put her iPod in the oven because she wanted hot tunes.

She asked for the number of 911.

She asked her doctor how long the 24-hour flu lasted.

She climbed over a glass wall to see what was on the other side.

She wanted to know how many One-A-Day vitamins to take.

She took the Pepsi Challenge and chose Skippy.

THE STATE OF THE KNOCK KNOCK JOKE

THESE JOKES KNOCK.

KNOCK KNOCK.
Who's there?
HAWAII.
Hawaii who?
HAWAII YOU? I'M DOING FINE.

KNOCK KNOCK.
Who's there?
ALASKA.
Alaska who?
ALASKA TO THE SCHOOL DANCE.

KNOCK KNOCK.
Who's there?
UTAH.
Utah who?
UTAH WOULD MAKE A GREAT COUPLE.

KNOCK KNOCK.
Who's there?
NEVADA.
Nevada who?
YOU NEVADA HAD IT SO GOOD!

KNOCK KNOCK.
Who's there?
TEXAS.
Texas who?
TEXAS ARE DUE APRIL 15TH.

KNOCK KNOCK.
Who's there?
MISSOURI.
Missouri who?
MISSOURI LOVES COMPANY.

KNOCK KNOCK.
Who's there?
NEW JERSEY.
New Jersey who?
MY NEW JERSEY'S FROM THE GAP.

KNOCK KNOCK.
Who's there?
WASHINGTON.
Washington who?
WASHINGTON OF LAUNDRY TONIGHT.

KNOCK KNOCK.
Who's there?
IOWA.
Iowa who?
IOWA DOLLAR FOR LUNCH MONEY.

KNOCK KNOCK.
Who's there?
MARYLAND.
Maryland who?
MARY, LAND THE PLANE OVER HERE!

KNOCK KNOCK.
Who's there?
MISSISSIPPI.
Mississippi who?
MISSISSIPPI IS MR. HIPPIE'S WIFE.

KNOCK KNOCK.
Who's there?
KANSAS.
Kansas who?
KANSAS GROUP OF KNOCK KNOCKS GET ANY WORSE?

EW, GROSS!

QUEASY DOES IT.

Ben: You're keeping a chimp in your gym locker! What about the smell?

Glen: Oh, he'll get used to it.

Did you hear about the pimply guy who was sent to detention hall?

He broke out!

What happened to the kindergartener who ate too much?

He tossed his cookies.

Why did the cannibal go to the football field?

He wanted to catch the last leg of the game.

What did the teacher say when his glass eye fell down the drain?

"Looks like I lost another pupil."

TOP 10 GROSS BOOKS

1. *The Baby-Spitters Club*

2. *The Princesspool Diaries*

3. *Nancy Drool Mysteries*

4. *Breaking Wind in the Willows*

5. *Winnie-the-Poo*

6. *The Barnacles of Narnia*

7. *Spew-art Little*

8. *Dear Dumb Diarrhea*

9. *The Molar Express*

10. *Spat the Bunny*

GROSS AND GROSSER

What is Mozart doing in his grave?

Decomposing!

What do you call 144 school lunches?

A gross

Linda: Teacher, Johnny didn't make it to school today because he was run over by a steamroller. What should I do?

Teacher: Slip him under the door.

KNOCK KNOCK.

Who's there?

ZIT.

Zit who?

THAT'S ZIT FOR NOW, FOLKS!

MUST-HEAVE TV:

Hurled News Tonight

MTV Mucus Video Awards

Desperate Houseflies

Throwing Up Brady

Entertainment Tonight

OVERHEARD AT THE CANNIBALS' HIGH SCHOOL REUNION

"How did you like the grads-u-ate?"

"You were always buttering up
the principal."

"Remember when our teacher got sick and
we had to cook with substitutes?"

"I feel sick. It must have been someone I ate."

"The chef sure makes a great meat loaf!"

"I became a waiter because
I like serving people."

"Remember when we creamed our
opponents?"

"Dinner's over. Everyone's eaten."

AMERICAN HISTORY TEST

IF YOU FLUNK THIS,
YOU'RE HISTORY.

1. True or false: George Washington's teeth?
They were false.

2. What did Christopher Columbus discover?
    a) America
    b) The "seven seas" on his report card
    c) Spanish explorers got more miles to the galleon

3. What kind of music did the Pilgrims enjoy?
    a) Plymouth Rap
    b) Plymouth Reggae
    c) Plymouth Rock

4. Why did pioneers cross the country in covered wagons?
   a) They were hoping to acquire unclaimed land.
   b) They didn't want to wait 50 years for a train.

5. The Boston Tea Party was known for its _____.
   a) tea shirts
   b) mocha lattes
   c) slammin' DJ

6. What didn't exist before Thomas Edison?
   a) Lightbulbs
   b) Lightbulb jokes
   c) If it wasn't for him, we'd be watching TV by candlelight.

7. Why did Lincoln walk seven miles to school every day?
   a) To learn his Abe B C's.
   b) Because he missed the bus.

8. The first American flag was _____.
   a) made by Betsy Ross
   b) just sew-sew

9. Why does the United States have a two-party system?
   a) To maintain a balance of checks and plaids
   b) So they can have one party on Friday night, and another one on Saturday night

10. During the Civil War, where did General Grant put his armies?
    a) In the Battle of Appomattox
    b) Up his sleevies

11. What did Paul Revere say during his midnight ride?
    a) The British are coming! The British are coming!
    b) Giddy-up!
    c) Give me a Minute, Man.

12. The Declaration of Independence was signed . . .
    a) at Independence Hall in Philadelphia.
    b) with a smiley face and circles over the i's.
    c) at the bottom.

13. The Louisiana Purchase . . .
    a) doubled the size of the United States.
    b) required an extra-large shopping bag.

14. What questions did the framers of the Constitution wrestle with?
    a) How can we safeguard democracy for future generations?
    b) Should Delaware her New Jersey?
    c) What style frame should we use?

15. We study American history . . .
    a) because our teacher won't let bygones be bygones.
    b) because, like our teacher, history is always repeating herself.
    c) so we can better understand joke books.

PRESI-DUDES THAT RULE

Which president had sharp teeth?

Jaws Washington

Which American president dug up bones on the White House lawn?

Rover Cleveland

Who was the first caveman president?

Ulysses S. Grunt

Which American president liked to trade?

Jimmy Barter

Which president liked a good pickle?

Dill Clinton

Which president needed to shave?

Hairy S. Truman

Which president had the most money?

Richer Nixon

Which president drove the carpool?

Martin Mini-Van Buren

Which president visited Norway?

Gerald R. Fjord

Which president worked at a gas station?

Millard Fill More

Who was the youngest president?

Babe Lincoln

NUTTY NUMBERS
BECAUSE SEVEN ATE NINE

Which movie star is good at math?

Add 'em Sandler

What did the calculator say to the student?

"You can count on me."

**Why did the geometry teacher open
the window?**

It was 360 degrees in there!

**Rick: I spent seven hours over my math book
last night.**

Nick: Why?

Rick: It fell under my bed.

What king invented fractions?

Henry the Eighth

Why do soccer players do well in math?

They know how to use their heads.

Why couldn't four and eleven get married?

They were under eighteen!

What do you get when you have 100 pennies, 25 nickels, and 15 dimes?

Droopy pants

Why did the algebra teacher excuse herself?

She had to go to the mathroom.

How many monsters are good at math?

None, unless you Count Dracula.

What did one decimal say to another?

"Did you get the point?"

What number has its own day?

Two's day

Teacher: If you add 6, 468, and 2,591, then divide the answer by 3 and multiply by 7, what would you get?

David: The wrong answer.

Math Teacher's Lunch Menu

Soup and Gram Crackers

Hot Coffee with

Half-and-Half

Three-Bean Salad

Clams on the Half Shell

Whole Wheat Bread with

Added Protein

Apple Pi

Toffee Squareds

Why are kindergarten teachers so optimistic?

They know how to make the little things count.

Why isn't your nose twelve inches long?

Because then it would be a foot

Why was the inchworm angry?

It had to convert to the metric system.

KNOCK KNOCK.

Who's there?

DIVISION.

Division who?

DIVISION IS DE JOB OF DE EYES.

KNOCK KNOCK.

Who's there?

LESS.

Less who?

LESS NOT HAVE HOMEWORK TODAY!

THE PRINCIPAL'S OFFICE
YOU'RE BUSTED.

Principal: You're suspended.

Paul: Well, I won't take this sitting down.

Principal: Why not?

Paul: These chairs are freshly painted.

Why did the clock go to the principal's office?

It was tocking too much.

The principal found out a student was forging her signature and charging other students. When she brought him into her office, she said, "I hope you have a good excuse for me." "I do," said the forger. "But it'll cost you."

Why did the father get sent to the principal's office?

He had a dad attitude.

Student #1: What are you in for?

Student #2: Running too slow in the hall.

Student #1: Don't you mean running too fast?

Student #2: No, I mean too slow.

The teacher caught me.

David: I don't want to go to school today, Mom. No one there likes me!

Mother: Well, you have to go.

You're the principal.

What does a school director take for a headache?

A princi-pill

Principal: Welcome to our school.

Transfer student: Thanks. Can you tell me what room I'm in?

Principal: The hallway.

Why don't schools cheat?

They have principals.

TOP 10 THINGS TO SAY WHEN YOU GET A BAD REPORT CARD

1. "Hey Mom: *C*'s are the new *B*'s!"

2. "That 50 in math means the size of the class."

3. "*F* is for 'fabulous.'"

4. "Those *C*'s and *D*'s aren't grades. They're vitamin deficiencies."

5. "On the other hand, I'm doing great in pig Latin."

6. "Now you won't have to sit through those boring award ceremonies."

7. "I told you I'd be going down in history."

8. "That's the last time I use a calculator from a box of cereal!"

9. "I didn't want to make the rest of the class look bad."

10. "At least I didn't get any *G*'s."

TAKE ME TO YOUR READER

SHHHHHH . . . YOU'RE AT A LIBRARY.

What did the librarian say to the book?

"Can I take you out tonight?"

Why did the boxer go to the library?

He wanted to hit the books.

How come the school library was so big?

They kept adding stories.

What did the librarian say to the noisy vegetables?

"Quiet, peas."

Librarian: What do you call the author of a western story?

A horseback writer

BOOKS YOU WON'T FIND IN THE SCHOOL LIBRARY

LOCKER AVALANCHE by Barry D'Alive

LION TAMING BY CLAUDE BOTTOM

Alone on the Bus by Bea O'Problem

Will He Graduate? BY BETTY WONT

The Smelly Locker by Jim Shortz

Always Tardy by Isabelle Ringing

Strange Disappearance by Warren D. World

ADMIRING MYSELF BY A. DONIS

SLIPPED ON THE HALF-PIPE by Major Y. Pout

Why did the book stop going to the library?

People kept checking her out.

Did you hear about the skunk who wrote a book?

It was a best-smeller.

Dan: Finished my book.

Stan: How long did it take you?

Dan: On the back it said 8 to 12 years, but I finished in a couple weeks.

Why did chaos break out in the library?

Someone found "dynamite" in the dictionary.

What do librarians wear outside?
Dust jackets

Librarian: Can you keep your voice down? The people around you can't read.
Girl: Really? I've been reading since I was four.

Librarian: Will you two please stop trading Pokémon cards?
Bob: We're not trading cards, we're playing video games.

Max: Where can I find a book about trees?
Library: Try the branch library.

Why do elephants have cracks between their toes?
So they can carry library cards.

MORE BOOKS YOU WON'T FIND IN THE SCHOOL LIBRARY

How to Write a Bestseller by Paige Turner

CARPOOLING STORIES BY MINNIE VAN

Daredevil Bungee-Jumping by Hugo First

Earn Money After School by Moe D. Lawn

Small Seats BY WILMA BUTFIT

School Drinking Fountains by Luke Warmwater

SUCCESS IN MATH CLASS by Cal Q. Later

HOW TO OPERATE A COMPUTER by Rita Manuel

EXCUSE ME, DO YOU HAVE THE RHYME?

What do you call . . .

. . . an instructor with two heads?

A creature teacher

. . . a student you can buy at the 99-cent store?

A dollar scholar

. . . a skateboard teacher?

A scooter tutor

. . . a street full of Mathletes?

A brain lane

. . . a library thief?

A book crook

. . . an exam-eating bug?

A test pest

. . . a Trojan horse?

A phony pony

GYM-NAUSEUM

What do soda cans take in school?

Fizz ed

Why do basketball players always have change for a dollar?

Every game is four quarters.

What did the school psychologist say to the cheerleader?

"You have a splits personality!"

Where do baseball players wash their socks?

In the bleachers

Did you hear the team bought new soccer balls?

Everyone kicked in.

Why didn't the nose make the football team?

It didn't get picked.

Why did the garbage collector's son get kicked out of the game?

He was talking trash.

Why did the football coach go to the bank?

To get his quarterback

How do you cool off at a football game?

Sit in front of a fan.

Why won't the surfer date the swimming teacher?

She was going out with the tide.

What do hockey players pledge allegiance to?

The United Skates of America

Why did the baseball player shut down his Web site?

He wasn't getting any hits!

Coach: Your baseball cap is on backward.

Kid: How do you know which way I'm going?

Why did the girls' baseball team wear stockings?

They had runs in them.

What did the soccer player say when he learned to ride a bike?

"Look, Ma — no hands!"

TOP 10 EXCUSES FOR LOSING THE BIG FOOTBALL GAME

1. We didn't want to clutter up the school's trophy case.

2. We had mystery tacos for lunch.

3. We forgot our lucky underwear.

4. The debate team beat us up.

5. We shouldn't have tried to join "the wave" during a play.

6. We wanted to finish the game so we could do our homework.

7. We wanted to get athletic scholarships for who we *are*, not how we play some silly game.

8. The walk to the football field took a lot out of us.

9. The coach turned into a pumpkin.

10. The guys on the other team kept trying to knock us down!

SPORTS SHORTS

Soccer player: I can't believe I didn't score — the goal was totally open! I could kick myself!
Coach: Why bother? You'd probably miss.

What do you do if your swimming class is filled?
Get on the wading list.

What did the policeman say to the swimming teacher?
"Can I see your diver's license?"

Student: The doctor says I can't play football.
Coach: I could have told you that.

Why did the baseball player bring a blanket to the game?
In case he had to cover first base

Frankenstein: I have the body of an athlete!

Dracula: Yes, and I think you should
give it back.

Why did the football player bring a rope to the game?

He wanted to tie up the score.

If a girl hockey player falls on the ice, why can't her brother help her up?

He can't be a brother and assist her, too.

Why couldn't the tennis player start a fire?

Because she lost all her matches

Why did the train go to the gym?

To join the track team

X-TREME SPORTS

What did the first-time skateboarder say to another?

"Can I crash at your place tonight?"

Why did the skateboarder lose the contest?

He was having a bad air day.

What do you call a skateboarding team that always wipes out?

The All-Scars.

Did you hear about the new surf movie?

It got *wave* reviews.

How does a teacher go surfing?

On a blackboard

KNOCK KNOCK.
Who's there?
TENNIS.
Tennis who?
TENNIS LESS THAN ELEVEN.

KNOCK KNOCK.
Who's there?
SOCCER.
Soccer who?
SOCCER IN THE ARM
SO SHE'LL STOP KNOCKING!

KNOCK KNOCK.
Who's there?
PITCHER.
Pitcher who?
PITCHER MONEY WHERE YOUR MOUTH IS.

KNOCK KNOCK.
Who's there?
TRAMPOLINE.
Trampoline who?
TRAMPOLINE ON THE LAWN IS NOT ALLOWED!

TOP 10 THINGS TO SAY TO GET OUT OF GYM CLASS

1. My gym suit is being dry-cleaned.

2. I already get tutored in gym.

3. Have you negotiated this with my manager?

4. I'm exercising my right not to exercise.

5. I have a sprained eyebrow.

6. I throw the bat when I play softball — I wouldn't want the school to get sued.

7. My doctor warned me against athletic-overuse injuries.

8. I've been diagnosed with Videogame Arm.

9. I've converted to a religion that forbids sweating.

10. Is smallpox contagious?

WORD TO THE WISE

Teacher: There's something wrong with your grammar.

Sam: Why? She's a nice old lady!

What's the longest sentence in the world?

Life imprisonment

Dumb: Our English teacher is pretty old.

Dumber: Why do you say that?

Dumb: She says she taught Shakespeare.

What do fish write in English class?

Brook reports

Did you hear about the kid with great penmanship?

He made straight A's.

Teacher: Can you make a sentence using the words defeat, deduct, defense, and detail?

Sam: Defeat of deduct jumped over defense before detail.

Teacher: What did you write your report on?

Sally: A piece of paper.

Sandy: I'm going to the cemetery to write my story.

Randy: Why?

Sandy: I need a good plot.

What do you get when you swallow an encyclopedia?

Inside information

Why did the hacker flunk English class?

He didn't know the password.

Did you hear about the car that wrote its life story?

It's an autobiography.

Teacher: Why is it so hard for you to learn how to spell?

Felicia: Because you keep changing the words!

Which whale had a big vocabulary?

Moby Dictionary

Jason: What does "coincidence" mean?

Spencer: Funny, I was just going to ask you that.

ARTSY-SMARTSY
PRETTY CRAFTY

What did the drawing say to the sculpture?

"Let's have an art-to-art talk!"

Why did the art student fail his test?

He drew a blank.

Why did the art teacher go to court?

Her painting was framed.

Did you hear about the artistic math teacher?

He liked to paint-by-numbers.

Art student #1: How did you paint such a good picture?

Art student #2: Easel-y.

What kind of painting did the Blob do?

A monsterpiece

Why did the boy leave his coloring book at the zoo?

He couldn't stay between the lions.

What do kids like to draw in school and listen to on the radio?

Car tunes

What's a ghost's favorite painting?

Moan-a Lisa

Why do vampires make boring art students?

Because they only know how to draw blood

HOW DID THEY DO IN SCHOOL?

—The linebacker?

He barely passed.

—The giraffe?

It got high marks.

—The bungee-jumper?

He was suspended.

—The worm?

It was at the bottom of its class.

—The barber?

He knew all the shortcuts.

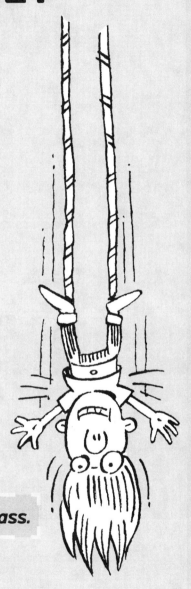

—The thermometer?

It picked up a few degrees.

—The lightbulb?

It wasn't very bright.

—The parachutist?

He dropped out.

—The jump rope?

It skipped class.

TOP 5 EXCUSES FOR HANDING IN YOUR ART PROJECT LATE

1. I can bring it to school, but first I'll have to insure it.

2. My work is so controversial, it was banned by the government.

3. How can you say a work of art is *ever* finished?

4. *Grade* it? I never pay attention to the critics.

5. My art project ate my dog.

MUSIC TO MY EARPHONES

THESE JOKES ROCK.

Bill: Our marching band is lousy.

Phil: Why?

Bill: Everyone is out of step but me.

Why did the dumb guy throw away his guitar?

It had a hole in the middle.

Why did the mummy try out for the school musical?

He heard there was a cast party.

Where can you find an alien with a trombone?

The Martian band

Music teacher: I'd like you to sing tenor.

Student: Really?

Music teacher: Yes, ten or twelve miles away.

How did the music teacher clean her teeth?

With a tuba toothpaste

Box office attendant: That's the sixth ticket you've bought for the school musical!

Kid: I know, there's a girl inside who keeps tearing them up.

Why did the music students get in trouble?

They were passing notes.

Peter: When I sat down to play the piano, everyone laughed.

Polly: Why?

Peter: No bench.

Why did the kid put his head on the piano?

He was trying to play by ear.

How do you fix an orchestra?

With a Band-Aid

Elephant: You said I could play in the school band.

Music teacher: No, I said when it comes to playing, you're banned.

Why did the music teacher get locked out of her classroom?

She had the wrong key.

Why did the thief want to be in the school musical?

So he could steal the show

What kind of music do whales like?

The blues

Why did the flute break up with the harp?

The harp was stringing her along!

What do you call a tuba player, trombone player, and drummer when it's a hundred degrees out?

A sweatband

Emma: How was that musical you went to last night?

Danny: Good, but I only saw one act.

Emma: How come?

Danny: The program said "Act Two — Three months later," so I went home.

MORE HOMEWORK EXCUSES

1. I got caught in a time warp, and handed it in five years ago.

2. My brother used it to line the gerbil cage.

3. Someone broke into our house and stole my math book.

4. My dog ate it, and then someone ate my dog.

5. An imaginary friend borrowed it and never gave it back.

6. I was busy filling out that teacher survey where I praised your performance.

7. Everything was lost when the meteor hit.

8. It was confiscated by Homeland Security.

9. It was sold on eBay.

10. My baby brother critiqued it, and it's still wet.

IT'S RHYME FOR A JOKE (AGAIN)

What does a hip math teacher use?

A cooler ruler

**What happens when
a smelly rodent doesn't study?**

The skunk flunks

What do you find at a school for fish?

A bass class

What do you get when erasers gossip?

Chalk talk

**What do you call a happy guy who's
completed school?**

A glad grad

What's a class celebration where everyone is late?

A tardy party

What do you call gossip during science class?

Lab blab

At school, where did young Mick Jagger keep his coat?

A rocker locker

What do you get when a copycat cleans out his desk?

A neater cheater

HOW TO MAKE HOMESCHOOLING FEEL LIKE REGULAR SCHOOL

PLEDGE ALLEGIANCE TO YOUR TEDDY BEAR.

WRITE GRAFFITI ON THE BATHROOM DOOR.

WEAR A GYM SUIT WHEN YOU PLAY KICK-THE-CAN WITH NEIGHBORS.

HOLD AN ASSEMBLY IN THE LIVING ROOM.

HAVE LUNCH ON A CRACKED PLASTIC TRAY. ASK FOR RUNNY SLOPPY JOES ON A STALE BUN.

CARRY ALL YOUR BOOKS IN A BACKPACK AROUND THE HOUSE.

ASK FOR A HALL PASS TO GO UPSTAIRS.

HAVE FRIENDS OVER FOR RECESS.

STICK CHEWED GUM WADS UNDER THE DINING ROOM TABLE.

SIGNS YOU NEED A VACATION

1. You install a hammock in your locker.

2. You toast marshmallows over a Bunsen burner.

3. Your answer to every math problem is SPF 45.

4. You do a book report on the *Rand McNally Road Atlas.*

5. You dissect a frog outside so you can work on your tan.

6. You cut the sleeves off your gym suit.

7. You pledge allegiance to the sun.

8. You keep a flotation noodle in your backpack "just in case."

9. You put Wite-Out on your nose so it doesn't get sunburned.

10. You take off your shirt and run through the school drinking fountain.

THE LAST DAY OF SCHOOL

What's the difference between the first day of school and the last day of school?

Nine months

What's the best part of school?

Summer vacation!

What's better than vacation?

More vacation!

Why did the boy get kicked out of camp?

He tried to steal answers to the swimming test.

Why did the small bucket go sunbathing?

It was a little pail.

Camp Counselor: Why don't you toast a hot dog?

Johnny: Here's to a great hot dog!

Why can't zombies go to sleepaway camp?

They don't sleep!

Bob: How did you find the weather on your vacation?

Rob: I just went outside and it was there.

Will: Why can't I climb a tree?

Mom: Well, if you fall and break both legs, don't come running to me!

SCHOOL'S OUT, LET'S SHOUT

What do frogs drink on a hot day?

Croak-a-cola

Why did the sailor run out to sea?

He got an urgent foam call.

Why did the mall rat go to the beach?

She heard there were buoys there.

What does the ocean do at a football game?

The wave

What happens to an air conditioner when you pull its plug?

It loses its cool.

Don: My grandmother came to visit during vacation.

Juan: Did you meet her at the airport?

Don: No, I've known her for years.

What's the best thing about Dracula's hotel?

Tomb service

KNOCK KNOCK.

Who's there?

CANOE.

Canoe who?

CANOE PUT LOTION ON MY BACK?

KNOCK KNOCK.

Who's there?

SANDAL.

Sandal who?

SANDAL GET IN YOUR PANTS IF YOU'RE NOT CAREFUL!

2 DUMB 2 B 4-GOTTEN

Some end-of-the-year yearbook-signing suggestions

You're the best friend
I ever made
in all three years
of seventh grade.

Won't be seeing you
for a while.
Please don't take me
off speed dial.

EVEN THOUGH YOUR WRITING'S SLOPPY,
I'LL MISS HAVING YOUR
TEST TO COPY

"To My BFF in the whole wide world!"
If I write this again,
I'm gonna hurl.

You tutored me in
English and math.
It didn't help —
I flunked the clath.

All year we've been
like peas in a pod.
Under my desk is
your gum wad.

I otter cry
I otter laugh
I otter sign
My otter-graph

A FEW SIGNS YOU'RE GOING TO SUMMER SCHOOL

You flunked lunch.

You sharpened the wrong end of the pencil.

At the PTA meeting, your parents denied knowing you.

Your report card was so bad, it was buried
in a toxic waste dump.

On the last day of class, your teacher says,

"See you Monday!"

SNAPPY SIGN-OFFS
HERE ARE A FEW WAYS TO SAY "HASTA LA VISTA, BABY!"

Yours Till . . .

. . . the ice screams

. . . the fire escapes

. . . the ski jumps

. . . the school dances

. . . the toilet bowls

. . . the banana splits

. . . the autumn leaves

. . . the pencil points

. . . the fire drills

. . . the milk shakes

. . . Niagara Falls

. . . the bed spreads

. . . the ocean waves

HOLLY KOWITT is the renowned author of jillions of books, including the bestselling *This Book Is a Joke* and *This Book Is a Joke, Too.* Her fondest school memory is appearing in the school health fair as the large intestine. When she isn't writing cannibal jokes, she likes to read, ride her bike, and check pay phones for loose change. She tests her jokes out on her nieces and nephews, who are punished if they don't laugh.